CW00742660

Do not fear, for I am with you,
do not be afraid, for I am your God;
I will strengthen you, I will help you,
I will uphold you with my
victorious right hand

Isaiah 41:10

Protect me, O God, for in you I take refuge.

Psalm 16:1

It is no longer I who live, but it is Christ
who lives in me. And the life I now live in the flesh
I live by faith in the Son of God, who loved me
and gave himself for me.

Galations 2:20

For I will restore health to you
and your wounds I will heal,
says the LORD.

Jeremiah 30:17

Blessed be the LORD,
for he has wondrously
shown his steadfast love to me.

Psalm 31:21

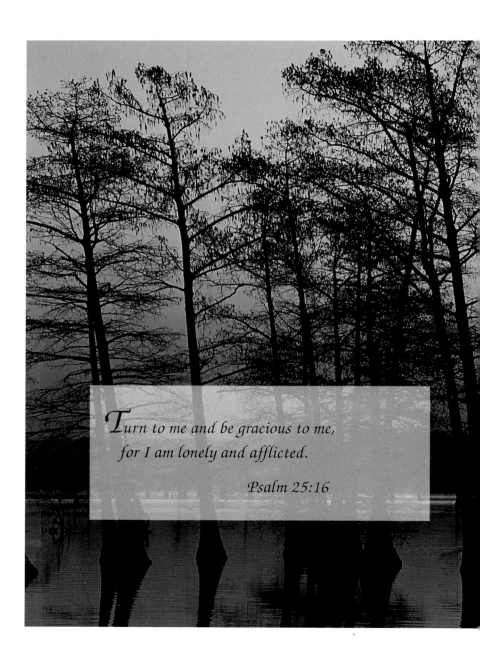

Turn to me and be gracious to me,
for I am lonely and afflicted.

Psalm 25:16

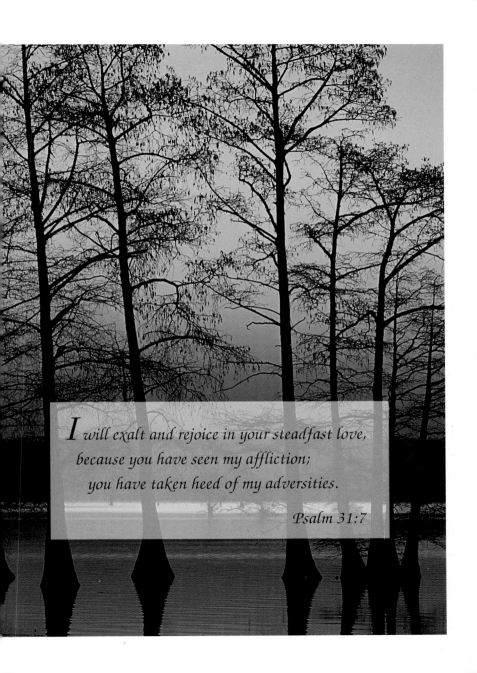

I will exalt and rejoice in your steadfast love,
because you have seen my affliction;
you have taken heed of my adversities.

Psalm 31:7

So I tell you, whatever you ask for in prayer, believe that you have received it, and it will be yours.

Mark 11:24

But you, O LORD, are a shield
    around me,
my glory, and the one who lifts
    up my head.

                            Psalm 3:3

So I will bless you as long as
    I live;
I will lift up my hands and call
    on your name.

                            Psalm 63:4

My soul melts away for sorrow;
strengthen me according to
your word.

Psalm 119:28

*W*ait for the LORD;
be strong, and let your heart
take courage.

Psalm 27:14

I will both lie down and sleep
   in peace;
for you alone, O LORD, make me
   lie down in safety.

Psalm 4:8

When my spirit is faint,
you know my way.

Psalm 142:3

Even though I walk through the
darkest valley,
I fear no evil;
for you are with me;
your rod and your staff —
they comfort me.

Psalm 23:4

British Library Cataloguing in Publication Data. A catalogue record for this book is available from the British Library.

Published by Eagle, an imprint of Inter Publishing Service (IPS) Ltd., St Nicholas House, 14 The Mount, Guildford, Surrey GU2 5HN.

All Scripture quotations are from the New Revised Standard Version of the Bible, copyright © 1989 by the Division of Christian Education, National Council of the Churches of Christ in the United States of America. Used by permission.

Special thanks to Susan Yarborough Jorjorian.

Byron Jorjorian has been capturing the natural world on film for twenty years. His photographs have appeared on nationally published greeting cards, calendars, brochures, magazines, video programmes, and advertising. Limited edition prints of his work can be found in businesses and private collections around the world.

Photography: Byron Jorjorian
Design and Layout: Nancy Cole
Printed in Singapore
ISBN 0 86347 266 4